Usborne

Farm Picture Puzzle Book

Illustrated by
Gareth Lucas

Designed by Ruth Russell
Written by Kirsteen Robson

The answers
are on pages
30–32.

13

15

21

25

ANSWERS

Cover

1

2-3

4-5

6-7

8-9

10-11

12-13

14-15

16-17

18-19

20-21

ANSWERS (continued)

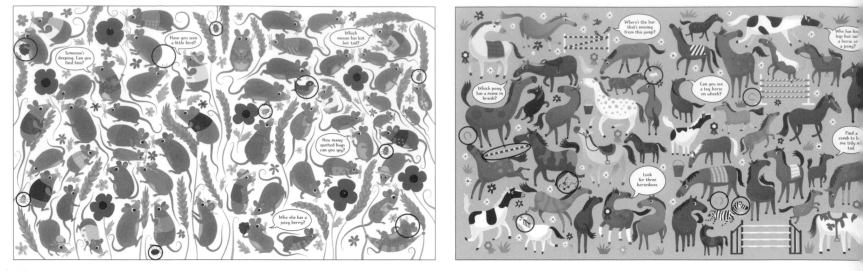

22–23

24–25

26–27

28–29